D1295923

DREAMS OF A SUMMER NIGHT

by the same author

*

COLLECTED POEMS, 1930–55
THE VIEW FROM A BLIND I
A VISION OF BEASTS AND GODS
EROS IN DOGMA

DREAMS OF A SUMMER NIGHT

by

GEORGE BARKER

FABER AND FABER
24 Russell Square
London

*First published in mcmlxvi
by Faber and Faber Limited
24 Russell Square London WC1
Printed in Great Britain by
Western Printing Services Ltd Bristol*
All rights reserved

PR 6003
.A69D7

© *Copyright by George Barker 1966*

CONTENTS

211216

THE SISTERON

Poem as dedication to Elspeth

The French window looks upon
those rocks and stones I have trod
with a lighter step today than when
I walked so many memories gone
the mountains of the Sisteron.

Where are those women of snow and swan
who seem to move beside me now
like may trees floating wildly on
the cataracts of recollection,
O mountains of the Sisteron?

So move beside me now these two
constructed as it were of flowers
a child and mother who renew
our love like poppies on fire on
the mountains of the Sisteron.

Yet still at night I dread the stars
conspiring to degrade the day
with a dark prognostication
in which again I walk alone
the mountains of the Sisteron.

But these two both by night and day
will lead me beside streams, and on
to the wild happy woods where they
and I shall find the golden way,
O mountains of the Sisteron.

Whether again I wander down
your bouldered slope or stride beside

that frolicking joker of the rock
the agile Durance, never again,
O mountains of the Sisteron,

Alone among the rock and stone—
(wild Alp of sheep and lavender,
white crag and shadowing conifer)—
I see with eyes that are not my own
the mountains of the Sisteron.

Eyes that are kinder far than mine
have given to me a vision
of natural absolution
like dawn unloading roses on
the mountains of the Sisteron.

High from its gold in the green sky
the noonday gazes dazzling down
on ringing meadows where we lie
hung in their hammocks by the sun,
the mountains of the Sisteron.

Or watch the evening flood the peaks
with shade that never before shone
such a nostrum and such peace
upon the conscience and upon
the mountains of the Sisteron.

For clouds that darker from the North
come riding the Alps and storm down
into these valleys, turn or seem
to turn to great doves dreaming on
the mountains of the Sisteron.

May thus all evenings, every one,
fall everywhere in such brightness on
those who have never known the sun
inscribe its absolving verb upon
the mountains of the Sisteron.

V MEMORIALS FOR DEAD FRIENDS

I

FORMAL ELEGY ON THE DEATH
OF OSCAR WILLIAMS

I

There by the stone in the short grass where, resting, you
    wait
with your spectacled eye turned on the road up which I
    approach you,
yes, I and all of us, sulking or shouting, some without
    gifts, and none late
and a few in the knowledge that if they should ever reach
    you
you will not, perhaps, be there, sad man of ashes, but gone
still further on seeking your republic of the elect:
and some come sober with excesses and some, not happy
    alone,
in processions of orgy like that Bacchanalian sect
who, cock-eyed and tiger-skinned dancing out of India,
    ride
astride their own backs to the grave; and some as to their
    home
walk truly up to the hot gate unhesitant, open-eyed,
unhelped by the three old hags—ah, wait there for a little
    time
by your stone, Oscar, and we shall meet as on many a
    former time.

II

Are the wraiths out there in the gardens where no summer
    storm
shakes them and no grief ever falls? Are those zany insom-
    niacs there
the unAmerican nightingales, and do they perform

nightly for you as never, you said, they did here?
And the mad sun you once saw like Jahweh's head in the
    sky
stuck on a ray of light, and prophetic with menaces,
burns it now there beside you, weeping from a crimson-
    lake eye
the pity you saw only in it and in no other face,
and was it, Oscar, your pity you saw in that face?

III

The dead are not dead as the stars or ideas die
so that nothing is left but ashes on time or the tongue;
their absences move about us like invisible eagles that fly
only just overhead so that we walk among
the benevolent empires of their jurisdiction, and even
when we are lost in the winter of Teutoburger
these eagles are not lost. To each of us is given
the two-headed eagle of a dead friend as augur,
and for us these eagles weep in the crystal of winter.

IV

How can I mourn, dear friend, when I think of you
    strolling
those high laurel-hung terraces your heart had so han-
    kered for
as you perched like a parrot up in your cage by Bowling
Green? And only the ghost of a dead wife to open the
    locked door
of your loneliness and lead you among us? I cannot mourn
when I think of that meeting at last with her whom so
    long
you hung around here awaiting your too long delayed
    return
to, she that dead wife whose only commission of wrong
was that she died before you. So may, at your re-union,

14

the earth not separate you two again where you sleep
in the American grave, each with your long lost com-
    panion,
but may earth hold you both closer and together keep
    you.

V MEMORIALS FOR DEAD FRIENDS

II

EPITAPH FOR JOHN MINTON

Rest, Johnny, rest, rest,
under the starry dirt
the lifelong daymare's past.
Shrieking the Harpies tear
and rend the breast apart
plucking and picking bare
what is left of the heart
but you will not be there
there in the empty bone
for the crisscrossrow nerve
and gutted skeleton
know that you are gone
know that your now is never
know that the joker's passed
know that at last at last
the flesh and furies must
leave you alone for ever
leave you alone at last.

V MEMORIALS FOR DEAD FRIENDS

III

MEMORIAL VERSES
FOR LOUIS MACNEICE

No, I never saw eye to eye
with this dead Ulsterman—
that face of a handsome sheep
like most of the Gaelic clan
seemed as though half asleep
until the drinking began:
yet somehow he managed to keep
his hands and his soul clean.

But what could I now hold
against this Irishman whom
no falsehood ever consoled
to whom no martyrdom
even remotely appealed,
and whose sense of freedom
moved only in the controlled
ironies of our doom?

And then, by accident,
we met and drank together
and I saw what was meant
by lyres of a feather:
I saw the reticent
nature that was either
too tender or intent
or disguised as neither.

Gentle MacNeice, excuse
those misconceptions that
once fell between us, those
(like taking the wrong coat)

errors that disclose
what is affectionate.
For God only knows
how hopeless our state
if it were not for those.

And I would like to think
whenever a pass or word
comes clean and quick as a wink
that you have overheard
and elevate your drink:
for, to be absurd,
by such jokes, I think,
your bones might be stirred.

I remember you said:
'All I have managed to learn'
and shook a fuzzy head
'is not to mix grape and grain.'
And at those words I heard
the sobersided turn
away, seeking instead
truths too big to discern.

Thus I would like to hope
the ironic Horatian
ode that in its scope
looks no larger than
a pocket telescope
taught your verse to scan
the lunatic face of Europe
with the eye of a man.

So, trusting that you now
hold the forgiving mood—
(I write this, anyhow,
most for my own good)

may the grass grow
greener where your blood,
Irishman, goes to show
others where you stood,
others how to grow.

V MEMORIALS FOR DEAD FRIENDS

IV

ELEGIACS FOR T. S. ELIOT

i

Since Eliot died in London yesterday
Evening the English language
Mourns her last gentle tyrant,
The English Church one of her higher
Advocates and the English nation
Its noblest American. Myself
I mourn an old friend, a mentor,
And the man of a moral example.
Now England must survive a loss
Already survived by New England
And Europe what England has lost.
To speak of him as I saw him, he was
Of the feline and mystery, like his own
Cats, very hard to arouse but even harder
To placate. I think the teeth of his soul
Faced inward, like those of the anaconda,
So that nothing he took to his heart
Or his soul could ever escape. Furthermore
I believe him to have been a spy of the gods
Disguising himself as publisher, policeman,
Verger and bankclerk, in order the better
To report on the state of the unreal city.
Now all his odd disguises are divested
And he stands before us for what he truly is:
A memory reminding us at all times
Of our responsibilities. Personally I
Take him to have been the Emperor Tiberius
Paying us a latterday visit down here
In order to see just how well we managed
Without him. Now not he, sadly enough,
But we shall know.

29

ii

As to the influence of this Lloyds Bank clerk
Upon the state of English poetry, I think
It was imperious. By this I mean
He restored to us what had almost gone,
The moral and intellectual porphyrogenitive.
And what had been, before his hegemony,
Expedience and a chaffering of poetic riff raff
Underwent, during his magistracy, the
Imposition of rigorous definitions
And that sense of spiritual onus
Inherent in all Pascalian interpretations.
Also he loved bad jokes.

iii

What is possible now is that things may get a bit out of
    hand
—the Greenwich meridian, for instance, shift a yard or
    two overnight,
or the colour grey, no longer subjected to his rigour, blend
for a lark with a hint of barefaced illegal delight
or the numeral 1 claim rather more than its right:

or that his effigy serenely sleeping there
in the Norman shadows of St Bartholomew's,
inexplicably and splendidly disguised as Rahere*
that devout joker, founder and priest, choose
to rise and bear a plate among the pews:

such misdemeanours seem perfectly possible now that
this far from hard hearted moralist has gone
into a Somerset grave, where, as like as not,
sitting, legs crossed, in shadow, almost but not quite
    alone,
he regards, with a smile, Rhadamanthus on his great
    throne.

* A resemblance which I have often noticed.

V MEMORIALS FOR DEAD FRIENDS

V

FUNERAL EULOGY
FOR ROBERT COLQUHOUN

Inscribed to Robert MacBryde

i

It was at four in the morning at work on his sketch of
  Death
He felt on his shoulder the tip of that twisting wraith
He had at last etched on the negative of his life.

As the flying Scotsman to the landscapes of the Pennine
  Chain
Or the Flying Dutchman to all illusions of the Ocean
So was Colquhoun to those through whom his devotion
  drove him.

What we saw was a winged engine illuminated with flame
Or the skeletal hull loom through the fog of our time
As he dominated and dogged the heart marked X.

I shall know him again by the self-graven epitaph in his
  face
When, as he may, he chooses to revisit this place
That gave him, as haven, little more than a grave.

Tenderest of men in the morning before the ravening
  ghouls
Swept out of his holyrood conscience like lost souls,
In the evening we heard him howling in their chains.

All things were, to this man, a sort of structural
Crucifixion, like the god of the straining pectoral
Brought down to the flayed stoat nailed to a tree.

I saw him with a single stroke so knife the nerve
Of a drawn form that in its convulsion it gave
Off life like a sigh and hung suspended there.

Aware long before we were aware that he was best dead
He waved his bony hand in a hieroglyph that said:
'I cannot rest. I leave the rest to you.'

And now this beautiful head and powerful hand
Which, between them, had so ennobled us, send
From nowhere the same message as before

When he taught us from the cell and through the bar:
'All things have been destroyed and therefore are
True subjects for their rebirth in our love.'

ii

By moonlight I see a stallion of Stubbs-Ucello
Gaunt, long-barrelled, yellow, lifting its head
Proudly out of a bunch of fallow thistle

Which is the Knoxian conception of Scottish
Responsibility. And now this proud man is dead.
This Highlander, this skinny Ayrman, this, yes, British

Mountaineer of spiritual violence
This draftsman who was not so much a painter
As the graphologist of our dying conscience,

Elected to go home to cold Kilmarnock
And render those he left behind a mere remainder,
For what he wanted lay north of Cape Wrath and the rock.

In the ferocious exhibition bout he conducted
With himself both Jacob and Angel, we, the audience,
Had at last become superfluous. We were subtracted.

34

I have to believe that, having contested the issue
With his own passion, he now resumes it in regions
To which neither our love nor our grief shall ever have
     ingress.

Intensity of spirit, that energy with which
Energy creates itself, is indestructible.
Now where is the wrestler Jacob meeting his match?

And, supernaturally, why? To that rigorous
Calvinist of the Image, canvassing the invisible
Icon in colours seemed at heart futile and frivolous.

What, I think, broke this horsebreaker of a man
Was the knowledge that not in things but in their dis-
     tances—
Yes, there the love that kills them always began.

Such a hero—and by this I mean
A heart that acknowledges the glory of consequences—
Foresees that the love that generates between

All things must in its own turn destroy them
Like rubbing hands of wood. What possible pretences
Existed for such a man? How could he employ them

In the already burning theatre of his spirit?
The consolation that pacifies those ashes
Is his. It is not ours. We cannot share it.

So let him lie now near the rock and the cold loch
Not to awaken again till Cape Wrath one day dashes
The last wave over that long grave in Kilmarnock.

AT THE BIRTH OF A CHILD

for Raffaella-Flora

Sacred fountain, let me find
at the genesis of our kind
some consolation of the mind.

On this dark November morning
the aureola of the dawn
like a golden child is born

so this day takes its origin
from impulses that begin
beyond the star we suffer in

and the babe steps from a cloud
where, before the heart's endowed
with all that's miserable, or proud,

there all creatures fraternise
and find in one another's eyes
the innocence that always dies.

This is that welcome of the stars
the lost and drowning sailor hears
like angels whistling at his ears

or the weeping caryatid
bowing down its heavy head
burdened with what it never did:

in the astrologies of night
they see that death is growing bright
with stars that never reach our sight.

And the cherubs of the day
redeem in their sacred play
the nightmare of our Succubae

as the infant of the breast
brings to those who cannot rest
the peace we had thought dispossessed.

It is the death of innocence
the cherubim of birth announce
on the trumpets of existence.

WILD DREAMS OF SUMMER
WHAT IS YOUR GRIEF

Wild dreams of Summer, what is your grief?
Wild dreams of Winter, what is your delight?
O holy day, O holy day, so brief
O holy day, before so long a night.

My love, my love, no, there is no waking
From that long bed or that sleep.
My love, my love, the heart is here for the taking,
And we can take, but not keep.

II POEMS WRITTEN NEAR LAKE NEMI

i

Ariccia, lovely valley, now
My sunrise and my sunset glow
Like fire along the Golden Bough

As in its lion cage the day
Lies down along the evening sky
With Venus sleeping in its eye,

Or crowing dawn up from the calm
Of each sleep sequestered farm
The cock shakes like a golden palm

And the Alban Hills stand round
hammering with the stroke and sound
like a harp hid in the ground.

The peasant climbs the morning hill
through treadmills of mimosa till
he seems to labour standing still

O lovely valley of mimosa
each of your holy days bestows
a love that gathers all things closer

and doves that gather in every tree
murmur between lake and sea
all the devotion within me

since like a cradle of the mind
here I or anyone can find
the love that nurses its own kind

because those lucky few whose birth
praised and is praised by this earth
know what such a love is worth.

ii

I rise and leave the shadows of the house.
The lake outside the window, in the evening
Takes on the crimson of the sunsetting heart
Transfixed at the centre of its suffering
By a single cypress like a fallen dart.

The doves shake in their cages and the wild
Grapevine hides among its own torn leaves;
The lizard, dead one moment, scintillates like
Lightning, and is gone. Everything grieves.
The day dies like rainbows in the lake.

Low in the sky a fingernail of moon
Lifts like a hand that rises from the grave;
I think all birds and beasts are silent in
The hanging fires of their exhausted love.
Now shades embrace. And the small deaths begin.

The chemistry of love so works in us
That we sweat flowers, and the air is changed
Into a sleeping seraph of the eye;
By this miraculous ceremony arranged
Night and day marry in the mottled sky.

Handmirror of Diana, emerald Nemorense
Like a moon fallen among the Alban Hills,
As green and deep as drowning seen in dreams,
I walk your grove until the evening fills
With voices that call to me from other times.

41

O Golden Bough, O sighing Golden Bough,
Hung like a lyre by this sacred lake,
Echo those times no more, echo no more.
Let the small bird so loud in shadows take
Wing and exult beside a happier shore.

WITH A WHISTLE UNDER A WINDOW

i

Beside the lake at noon
I stand and see the sun
burning the water up
in a rock crystal cup
and as I look I see
more than I can behold
Miranda O Miranda
every fish is gold.

ii

She is to me
what the sea
is to the shell:
the life I breathe, the love
in which I dwell.

iii

The kingdoms of the Queen
and all the Earls of Grief
who mourn what might have been
the love so brief so brief
no, never ever green
but faded on the leaf
before it brought to life
the babe that burns between
these two nailed out upon
the saltire of what must be
and what can not be done:
there by that golden bough
as they lie down in love

the kingdoms of the Queen
and the last Earl of Grief
there by that golden bough
as they lie down in love
how can they know enough
to leave the clamorous bone
to live for ever alone
and let it die of love?
For when the heart turns to stone
then the amorous heart
knows that for their part
these two die into one.
And so the womb starts
to atone for the death of the heart
and all the wrong done
by the last Earl of Grief
and kingdom of the Queen.

THE STABAT MATER

The sorrowing mother was
standing beside the cross
   her son died on
as through her heart of hearts
pain like a flock of darts
   flew sobbing in.

O such affliction then
the mother of this son
   knew as she saw him,
she trembled where she stood
felt her own flesh and blood
   rush to adore him.

Who is the one will not
weep to see all that
   this woman suffers?
who without compassion
look on the immolation
   that she offers?

She saw her son rejected
her own son whipped and tortured
   for all men;
she saw him hang in torment
till at the holy moment
   he lived again.

Fountainhead of sorrow
O mother teach me also
   to love as I mourn,

tender me so much of
your sorrow and your love
    that my tears burn.

And, mother, grant that I
may seem also to die
    on my own cross
and let me also share
those wounds I cannot bear
    since they are his.

I gather my grief with
the tearglass of the truth
    and hope I may give
for that man crucified
tears not to be dried
    as long as I live.

Virgin of virgins, be
turned not away from me:
    grant I may bear
his death within me so
that I may also know
    how to die here.

Burning and burning, by
you, virgin mother, I
    beg to be sheltered
when at the Day of Wrath
by that tremendous death
    everything's altered.

Virgin and queen of virgins
when that last day begins
    O let me see
the dawn break on his face
and let his breath like peace
    be borne upon me.

Grant me the shadowing
hand of his harrowing
   nailed out on wood
and fortified underneath
the crosstree of his death
   stand where you stood.

And when the flesh is dead
heaven from overhead
   send down to me
out of the holy skies
the bird of paradise
   from you to me.

TO THE MEMORY OF ELROY FLECKER

'November eves! November eves!
They used to cloak Lockhampton Hill'
The fog descends. The smoking leaves
Cackle the same old moral still:
Everything that dies believes
It goes on living. And it will.

I join you, long dead never dead
Friend stalking through the autumn gloom,
Hollow-eyed Philhellene who led
My boyhood out of a schoolroom
Out to the golden seas and said:
'Your snails have towers, I presume?'

All evening let us walk that shore
Where the voice echoes a thousand years,
Or so you said. After two score
Faintly like seashells at my ear
I hear the spectre singing on the shore.

DREAMS OF A SUMMER NIGHT

I

What was the date of that day when, unbefriended by any
Of those who had preceded us, without advice from the
      gods,
Who sulked as usual in their tents of vanity,
Cold and not wholly convinced of the purpose of our
      journey
We set out for whatever it is we find at the end of the day?
And why should that date matter? It matters because the
      rogation
Of all ceremonial knows, when it reaches full circle
Then its purpose is done, as when the praying wheel
      slowly
Rides to its point of rest with a last supplicatory sigh.
I do not know the purpose of this journey, or even
If in the end it reaches a purpose, and have no desire to
      know, for the prospects
Are so wholly marvellous in themselves that to contem-
      plate
Them is enough. The little house on the mountain
Where a hero was born with a ploughshare in his left fist
      and
A new word for love in his mouth, the painted and shal-
      low springs of the Umbrian
Who loved white oxen, the ruined sea-palace of a black
      king
Visible only to angels and aeroplanes and the incurious
      rainbowfish,
And, O Calabria, those white beehive small farmsteads
To which, as it seems, the dignity of man has at last
      retreated
Awaiting another defeat: such an enumeration
Of almost sacred instances is always a personal litany
And enough is enough for the day. Thus in the evening

211216

We know that whatever has happened may, in itself,
    comprise
The complete supplication. And the sigh
Of the heart as it closes its blowzy old rose for the night
    could
Well be the smile of the holy wheel as it comes to rest.

II

To you, then, still asleep on a holy hill, I send
Such a word as this to alight at your half-open window
And awaken you with explanations, as below you, the
    sunrise
Explains itself to the Tiber in a series of golden reflections.
Thus, if I am fortunate, I may find some words prepared
    to
Bare themselves down to their bones and even to their
    family secrets:
For all words, and all objects, particularly the most
    commonplace, carry
Invisible robes of theology on their shoulders (and often
Not so invisible) as when the ordinary terracotta flower-
    pot
Wears its domestic humility as though it conveyed down
    the ages
Some property as sacred as the vessel of Joseph conveyed
Like a rose perpetually recurring. No, things are never as
Simple as they seem, but I do know, even in dreams,
That when we gaze at the masked diorama of objects
What we are really contemplating is the liturgy
Within appearances, like the bread and the body. Then
    in this liturgy
Those transcendentals are trapped that no other con-
    ceivable

Configurations can ever reveal to us. (Was this why
    Saint Dominic
Tore off the little bird's feathers?) Thus the gods inhabit
Every machine. And this secret, this dreaming religion
That lies sleeping within all things can be awakened
Like you, only by love in a hand, at whose touch, like a
    water diviner's
The rose rises up through her stalk and the handmirror of
    Diana
Unveils her moon and lake face. Asleep within the word
The poem lies dreaming. From the heart's cleft rock
    ascends then
The dove that truly exonerates all passion and liberates
    every Prometheus from
The unspeakable chains of our silence.

Can I believe such a word I send to you?

III

When the majority looks out of its moral citadel
Does it smile upon us, we whom it knows to be only
The oddfellow gardeners, the slightly drunken eccentrics
    with
Manias about outmoded machinery like honour,
The mutual duty of creatures afraid of each other to
Forgive what they fear, and an obsession with loneliness?
To this giant of majority whose home is a cave
In which hang the hearts, the hands, the dreaming heads
Of those victims whose sacrifice, like caryatids, supports
    the citadel,
To this Polyphemus what shall we answer, save in a
    whisper,

'No man.' And the scapegoat, weeping huge tears in the
    wilderness,
Turns and looks backward upon the scenes of its child-
    hood
Knowing only too well that though it believed it was
    once
Loved in its own home, it never, no never, was.
So too in derelict allotments one hears the crying, the
    shouting
Of those children who do not know that they are begging
Among the fallen ceilings and the broken beer bottles and
    the debris
For a hand to gather them and a step to lead them home
    to
The sacred hearth. And then, as I hear them, I remember
That Polyphemus is us, and the sad monster who rages
Weeping in his cave and wilderness, outcast, pariah,
Rejected, the ontological scapegoat of destiny,
Tossing the twisted horns of those morals upon which it
    is tossed,
This Prometheus of majority, this giant whispering on
    the fiery rocks,
Cries out at last to a greater monster with one eye:
'O Everyman.'

IV

From whom save those who sleep in a strange cloud
    beside us—
The acanthus entwining their limbs like heart-leafed
    involvements and the
Promise bruising their parted lips as they breathe it so
    lightly
That the butterflies alighted on their eyelids never even

So much as stir—from whom save them can we always
Evoke the forgiveness that exacts even more torment?
I am brought to these effigies that dream at the Tomb of
    Pompey
By that path through the park where, in the evening rain,
I walked with a friend in November, and saw, under the
    trees
Shadowed and silhouetted in the patterned moonlight,
Spellbound, the lovers. Then the raincloud suddenly
Obscured the moon, and in the rain and the darkness
I heard the moaning of those who are so hopelessly
    chained together
That they walk in each other's dreams, and, in torment
    together,
Cry out in a hideous joy as they burn to ashes
Like the bird in the fable of fire. For the head of Pompey,
    dreaming
In those serene gardens set between lakes and a sea,
Forgets as it mourns that all it has lost is the mystical
Body of loving and of suffering.

V

High on a hill in Wales with friends when the sun was at
    midday
I sat eating an apple and saw what lay below me—
The green and gold checkerboard of farms and fields that
    rolled to the
Hills of the west, and a twist of road in a valley
Hissing and silver in the noon and a redhanded sportscar
    racing up
Into its own unfashionable future—idly I saw them
All sliding like thoughtless swans on water into that
    August afternoon

And a benevolent evening. But then, like a toy from a
　　box, neat as bricks,
The black and white chapel set in its cemetery of some
　　forty gravestones
Caught and captured my speculation. And
'These without wishes or friends,' I thought, 'they have
　　their future already
Sleeping in that quiet valley where nothing unexpected
　　can wake
Them and of all this landscape they alone are not part
　　since
They cast no shadows, they have their homecoming, and
　　the golden silence they dream in
Is spread by a holier sun, never, like ours, due to set.'

VI

I think of her where she lies there on her stone couch by
　　the Thames
With the winds of the world asleep among her shrouds
　　and the gales
Hushed in her furled sails and the pawing white seahorses
At last at rest around her and the mermen of yesterday
　　calling to her
From the wind tossed reach of the river as it sweeps
　　through Greenwich
Meridian. I think of her as I think of a seagull caged in
　　chains but
Still standing poised, prepared, wings lifted, for the rise
　　and veer
Into the sunrise of Asia as far as the paradise islands of
The Coral Sea. And below her decks all the great figure-
　　heads fraternising

Like kings and queens at a feast—the Cleopatra, the
    Lallah Rookh,
Abraham Lincoln, Thermopylae, the American Officer,
Diana and Marianne, filling her hold with the dialogues
Of storms and calms, of long summer days and seas
Murmuring in their dreams, all these join with the voices
Of the dead sailor still roped at the chained wheel and
The ghosts that lean singing into the bitter wind that
    drives up from
The thundering graves of the sea.

VII

Dreams of a summer night when I rose before dawn and
    sought you
In acacia'd gardens with such an exuberance of blossoms
That it might be, I thought, they multiply round me in
    darkness—
Down a stone stair that led to the sea I remember
    descending
Following, as it seemed, some Persephone, some familiar,
Some friend unknown to me who moved in silence before
    me
Until I could hear the Tyrrhenian scarcely stirring at my
    foot—
O Stella Maris! Who were you who walked there before
    me
Down to that water without ever turning to see whom
You had wakened out of his dreams and brought to the
    sea?
O Star of the Sea, you were my only too fugitive hope that
Exoneration at the great founts may be found for
All we have suffered and all we have caused to suffer.

Ah, had I advanced one step into those glittering reaches,
    I
Believe that, for a moment, I might have received all
All of your exculpation. Dreams of a summer night,
Lakes breaking through sacred trees and always deserted
    gardens
And the presence of absences seeming to seek an unattain-
    able consolation,
The fading and far voices of children raised in their
    unavailing cry for love,
O Dreams of a summer night, why must such memories
    rise
Eclipsing the Star of the Sea and all expiation?
I turn and ascend the stone steps as, behind me, I hear
The unforgettable intercession of the summer Tyrrhenian
That promises to forgive: but turning to believe, I see
Only the starless midnight and the glittering of my
    illusions.

VIII

Star O star of the sea
Walking upon the water
Your blind vision has brought
A branch of the dove to me:

For what I never knew
Is that the soul lives
In peace only when it forgives
What it can not undo.

IX

I saw this villa set in a garden of arbours and bowers
Of immense decaying roses and a grapevine long un-
  tended;
Tall weeds had invaded the paths and, hanging by rusty
  nails
The trellis work, broken, seemed to regret a hand that
  was gone. There
By a half-open French window, standing in a white trance
  of silence
I saw one whom I loved cradling asleep in her arms
One whom I loved, and though no chill wind shuddered
The decaying roses or clattered the broken shutters,
Though no bough stirred,
Though no tall weed hissed and no grapevine trembled,
I knew that a zephyr of death had entered that garden
And that no one else would ever enter that garden.

X

Pines and serene skies and a morning sea so placid that
it lies calm and green as though it had turned to a lake,
and three fishermen with a net looped like a lace curtain
caught in a motionless dance, and, far away over that
  still sea
mounting out of the haze and horizon frieze of dawn
clouds like the rampant Pegasus of morning, pawing up,
  over
the fly of a fishing boat far, far out: O morning shores of
  Fregene
can you retain for ever the names that I wrote in your
  sand?

Long seabeach of Fregene, almost deserted in the September evening,
still remembering in dreams the deathfires of far-off Lerici,
an enormous autumnal sun resting upon your horizon at
that breathtaking moment of hesitation before it is suddenly gone,
and always the two masterless dogs lolloping side by side
after a figure that never again walks your silver shore,
O long seabeach of Fregene, almost deserted in the September evening,
will you be haunted for ever by the memory of my little sons?

XI

To find that the house really stands there under tall trees
With a field and a small bridge to the right and, to the left,
Where, as I knew it would be, the walled garden of peaches
Never closes its old door to intruder or visitor, there
I came at last upon the house that I knew was truly the past.
On the lawn the old colonel and his lady sat, she with a book and
He dozing in a deckchair with a shabby cocker spaniel beside him
And all their dead friends standing with teacups in their hands
Around them, recalling those summers long gone before emperors
Retired into libraries and the heroic goldenhaired soldiers

All died in that dirty valley of passion. Do the gods look
 down
On this little tea party taking place in the daydreams of
An ageing colonel as he dozes in a later August
And whisper: 'Yes, we were wrong'? Some of the dead
 who
Stood chatting in groups on the lawn in their outmoded
And beautiful finery seemed to know that in death a
Splendour invested them which no life could ever
Ever have imparted to them, that their destiny was
 hereafter to
Stroll on a terrible stage in a dumbshow perpetuating
Their otherwise fated, their fleeting, their almost forgot-
 ten
Memory. Admonished by these spectres we remember.

As I approached the Colonel stood up and extended his
 hand to me
Out of the past, and I held it not briefly, knowing that
Sometimes, but only too seldom, we can take tea with the
 dead.

XII

No, voices of captains and poets long dead, I shall not
 attend to your
Clamour in the laurel tree outside a door you dare
Never re-enter, for this is the house of life, where
You have no place, only echoes, only a rumour
Remembers you and your cobweb-invested and posthu-
 mous victories.
Peace, importunate speechless corpses, return to the
 silence of

Poor Pompey's Tomb stuck away in that garden at
   Albano
Unvisited save by sweethearts who neck on the public
   benches
Over your famous skulls and mock you with vicious
   tongues.

In the gardens of life I hear the swansinging dead.

XIII

Driving through October mists that Sunday afternoon it
   was as though
I traversed deep lanes through woods of my memory until
The sigh and hiss of the car seemed like Time reversed
   and the hill
Revealed not a prospect to come but one that had gone.
I saw moving in mists the recollection of friends whom
   only one journey
Will ever restore to us, I saw boys fishing in dreams
Who could not answer the call I could not give.
Sheep wandered up from a childhood and stood mutely
Accusing perhaps me of forgetting that we, too, had once
Brushed against one another near a gate in a field long
   ago.
Sometimes a birdcall echoed a note that I knew
Rose from an old lilt sung with a friend long before so
Much of the Teme had borne so many under
That angled stone bridge at Ludford. A hidden lane
Chose of a sudden to open itself as I passed and
I saw the three figures in raincoats disappear as
A shaking of leaves changed the shadows. Then the moon
   rose

Over Wales and I saw that my own face, white in the
    windscreen,
Stared back at me as though it glared at a ghost.

XIV

Out of the cold and hardened heart
    Such ghosts and roses teem
Such images and memories start
    As from a desert dream:

How can I cast that brittle gourd
    Like a dead thing away?
From its old husk such seas have poured
    As to sweep worlds away.

XV

Never by those whom the powers that be have ordained
    to destroy us
Shall we in the end be destroyed but rather by those
Destined to succour us in the instant or year of affliction.
They cast us the rope as we go down for the third time
    and
It sings as it throttles; they tender a cordial glass to
The love that lies bleeding and always the cup is full of
Crushed mirrors, diamonds, and the death of Lorenzo de
    Medici:
The kiss they lean over to calm with always excites the
Heart to its last wild gallop and implants upon
Those eyes that it loves the coins of the dead

Stamped with the face of Eros. No nostrum exists for
The ineffable disease of their absence when they with-
     draw to
Gather that nostrum, and, after the ball is over,
Whose severed head is adored on the dressing table?

XVI

Little Assisi of a November evening with torrential rain
Sweeping across that deserted square where so many have
     stood
With their suitcases full of hope and their hopeless hearts
As empty as this square in the November evening,
Suddenly a violent gust of east wind shudders across as
I retreat to a bar and stand staring back at
That arched and haunted rectangle crowded so full of
     shadows
All hoping for a little hope, that for a moment it seemed I
Stood at the iron gate of Hell and heard
All the about to be hopeless exhaling their last sigh of
     hope
Here in Assisi. And the cold wind ferociously
Drives them with whips of sleet like leaves into the dark-
     ness
Hissing and twisting and sighing. So near that sweep and
     flurry
Hoping against all hope I stood at the bar.

XVII

Mosaic'd saints whom no compassion has ever visited,
    tall in
your architecture of echoes, cave-eyed and gilded like
    fallen
kings, I hear in your iron cathedrals the whispering of
    lonely
seas near archipelagos no one but you has ever known.
Like the caged polar bear down whose great visage in
    springtime
I have seen huge tears slowly descend, I see the day-
    dream
harking for those far islands in your dark eyes,
those Lindisfarnes rising and sinking at the antipodes
the holy islands to which only an oakleaf can trans-
    migrate
you on the breath of the word. And the cenobite
herons cry happily at your return, they stalk down the
    crystal hills
to pick the tears from your eyes with their elegant bills.
From the cave of your vision and the Jeromeless
years the golden-tongued lion, save for your love home-
    less,
lopes up to greet you on that marvellous shore
and stands there with your open book hooked in his paw
like a gift, and in the sky an extraordinary host
of doves with vertical wings like scissors announce that
    lost
love has returned at last.

What are those far islands O saints whom no compassion
    has
ever visited and whither like winter swallows from June
    seas

you must return? What seabound rocks are those
whispering among the pitiless Capes of No Hope? And
   whose
mystery draws you home? O holy effigies
staring from starry domes with blind enamelled eyes
and no hearts at all, they are the islands of Pity
that out of the doomsday rock of sanctity
you hark for, and when you step down from your dome
Pity is the wind that will waft you home.

XVIII

The shades of childhood
Rise before me
Turning away their
Forgotten faces
But still I see
Like a glass of tears
The eyes of childhood
Gaze upon me.

Why do they turn
Away from me
Every wild one of
My shades of childhood?
Each seems to see
The ghost of its conscience
Like a white presence
Standing by me.

Then who tell me who
Ah who are they
The forgotten faces

Mopping and mowing
In Time like a tree?
Foretelling foreknowing
All the sad stories
That are now the memories
Of what had to be.

Is it I or you
O shades of childhood
I hear mourning in
Time like a tree?
O angel shades
Rise up and cover
Our eyes so that we
Cannot see.

Never no never
Ever return to
That wild wood
Where like larks
We once rose and sang
O shades of childhood
Crowd now around me
As here in my heart our
Shadows hang.

I hear them sighing
Like voices that fade
When the song is over
As shade after shade
Falls away from me:
O shades of childhood
Farewell for ever.
Remember me. O
Remember me!

XIX

The singing robe is a mantle of fire in which
What is dead, what is gone, is reborn from its own ashes
(Arise, some avenger!) like a corpse strolling about the
    streets
In the horse-shoe wreath and the polished shoes
Of its own burial. And, as every hour adds a small death
To our ever decreasing longevity, until all that is left is
    a bone, so
The poetic seizure, like that of sexual love, is to die
Each time more than a little of the briefly allayable fever:
That of excessive being. Out of this too-multiplying a
    rosetree
Of spiritual passion the wreath and ring o' roses then
    arises
To adorn its own death as the swan crowns itself with a
    requiem.
Ah, there is something that dies
In the spirit whenever the spirit conceives.
Not only the Virgin with her hand on the Unicorn's horn
    and
Not only the Infant of our own innocence to this oblation
Offer themselves up, but, worse than this, the
Hope at the heart of all sacrifice dies a little whenever
A god is not born from our ashes. Then Apollo in his
    deathcell
Inscribes with a finger of fire on the wall of the poem
Those words no Virgil has ever repeated, that death not
    yet avenged.

XX

My own little dove, my own little dove,
  The summer, now, is over
And the long golden age it gave
  Gone down to dust for ever—

Save that, like goldenrod in the ground,
  Next summer lies awaiting
O my own little dove, the revisiting sound
  Of your wings, and its waking.

XXI

In the stony recesses of the mind madness lives like a
    holy man
Happy among rocks and lizards, companion of worms and
    jackdaws,
Teacher of bats, instructor of trolls, Master Dancer of all
The mopping and mowing demons who never absent
    themselves from
Those obscene orgies we hold in the Holy of Holies where
Lounging in clouds of Circean drowsiness
The soul sings to herself of Liberty. I have seen
That stripdance of manic shadows in their St Vitus of life
Shaking the last vestment of responsible sorrow from
    their shoulders
Step out of the sawdust corpse and agonised ego in dark,
And then sit smiling in a lotus of joy at ceasing to mean.

'What is holy in this madness is that we have
Divested ourselves at last of the love of all created things,
    yes,

69

Even the creature that loves,
And broken like butterflies out from the husk of what is
Into a dazzling existence where we can dance all day
Before the marvellous tabernacle of categories without
    imperatives
And so become holy by leaping out of (even our own)
    nature into
The palm of the Great Illusionist and Psalmist.'

XXII

Those dreams of Medusa's head hung there in the hand
    of the hero
Who shall reveal them? 'I was the housedog petrified in
    its
Pompeiian convulsion, I was the babe born in the hotbed
    of the Abomination
And the ship howling in darkness and the anarchic sea
Cropfull of hands. I was the pitiless regard of heaven
Turned upon these things with never a tear mystifying
Its indifferent eyes. I was my shadow smiling up from
    Death Valley and
Hypnotised, chanting a paean in praise of destruction,
Death, dereliction, destruction. I was the City of London
    in flames with, overhead, virgins
Plucking their psalteries and saints contemplating their
    navels.
I was the engines of Justice rusting in the skies of sunset
And armies asleep dreaming of peace. I was tempests
Gathering in thunderheads over the heart's red sea and
Ah, I was lightning dividing it.' Agonised head of Medusa
Greater degradations await you, the keys uncrossed and
    the flaming
Gates that prevail as Armageddon uncoils from its sleep

And instead of the sun a dragon of hydrogen rises up in
     the Orient.
Thus I take you, dreaming head, in my hands where you
     lie
Cast away by the hero, rejected by anthropologists, dis-
     carded
By all save those who eavesdrop on your nightmare,
And lift your whispering death's-head from the floor-
     boards
Of my small room here in Islington. I gaze into the still
Living and petrifying eyes and kiss the chill
Grave of your lips. I hear you, as in a dream, Medusa,
     moan:
'I am the sorrow that turns the heart to stone.'